50 Turkish Dinner Recipes for Home

By: Kelly Johnson

Table of Contents

- Köfte (Turkish meatballs)
- Karnıyarık (Stuffed eggplant)
- İmam Bayıldı (Stuffed eggplant with tomatoes and onions)
- Lahmacun (Turkish pizza)
- Pide (Turkish flatbread)
- Kuzu tandır (Slow-roasted lamb)
- Etli yaprak sarma (Stuffed grape leaves with meat)
- İskender kebap (Turkish doner kebab)
- Kuzu şiş (Grilled lamb skewers)
- Adana kebabı (Spicy minced meat kebabs)
- Börek (Savory pastry filled with cheese, meat, or vegetables)
- Menemen (Turkish-style scrambled eggs with tomatoes and peppers)
- Kuru fasulye (Turkish white bean stew)
- Şiş kebap (Marinated meat skewers)
- Tavuk şiş (Grilled chicken skewers)
- Etli pilav (Turkish meat and rice pilaf)
- Çılbır (Poached eggs with yogurt and spicy butter)
- Patlıcan kebabı (Grilled eggplant kebabs)
- Mercimek çorbası (Turkish lentil soup)
- Hünkar beğendi (Lamb stew served over creamy eggplant puree)
- Balık köfte (Fish meatballs)
- Kuzu tandır pilavı (Rice pilaf with lamb)
- Kuzu güveç (Lamb stew cooked in a clay pot)
- Tavuk sarma (Stuffed chicken rolls)
- Zeytinyağlı yaprak sarma (Stuffed grape leaves with rice)
- Karışık kızartma (Mixed fried vegetables)
- Şakşuka (Turkish vegetable stew)
- Közlenmiş biber salatası (Roasted pepper salad)
- Patlıcan salatası (Eggplant salad)
- Haydari (Yogurt dip with garlic and herbs)
- Cacık (Turkish yogurt and cucumber dip)
- Hummus (Chickpea dip)
- Tarama (Fish roe dip)
- Ezme (Spicy tomato and pepper relish)
- Acılı ezme (Spicy tomato and pepper dip)

- Patlıcan ezmesi (Eggplant dip)
- Mücver (Zucchini fritters)
- Sigara böreği (Rolled phyllo pastry filled with cheese or herbs)
- Kabak mücveri (Zucchini pancakes)
- Kısır (Turkish bulgur salad)
- Fırın patates (Oven-roasted potatoes)
- Semizotu salatası (Purslane salad)
- Fasulye piyazı (White bean salad)
- Meze tabağı (Assorted appetizers platter)
- Peynir tabağı (Assorted cheese platter)
- Şekerpare (Turkish semolina cookies soaked in syrup)
- Baklava (Layers of phyllo pastry filled with nuts and honey)
- Künefe (Turkish cheese pastry soaked in syrup)
- Revani (Semolina cake soaked in syrup)
- Lokma (Turkish fried dough balls soaked in syrup)

Köfte (Turkish meatballs)

Ingredients:

- 500g ground lamb or beef (or a combination of both)
- 1 onion, finely grated
- 2 cloves garlic, minced
- 1/4 cup fresh parsley, finely chopped
- 1 teaspoon ground cumin
- 1 teaspoon paprika
- 1/2 teaspoon ground black pepper
- 1 teaspoon salt, or to taste
- 2 tablespoons olive oil (for brushing or frying)
- Optional: 1/4 cup breadcrumbs (to help bind the mixture)

Instructions:

1. In a large mixing bowl, combine the ground meat, grated onion, minced garlic, chopped parsley, cumin, paprika, black pepper, salt, and breadcrumbs (if using). Mix well until all the ingredients are evenly incorporated.
2. Once the mixture is well combined, take small portions of the mixture and shape them into small balls or elongated patties. You can wet your hands slightly to prevent the mixture from sticking.
3. Heat the olive oil in a skillet over medium heat. Once hot, add the köfte in batches, making sure not to overcrowd the pan. Cook for about 4-5 minutes on each side, or until browned and cooked through. Alternatively, you can grill or bake the köfte.
4. Once cooked, transfer the köfte to a serving plate and serve hot with your choice of accompaniments, such as rice, bulgur pilaf, salad, yogurt, or tomato sauce.

Enjoy your homemade Turkish köfte!

Karnıyarık (Stuffed eggplant)

Ingredients:

- 4 small to medium-sized eggplants
- 300g ground lamb or beef
- 1 onion, finely chopped
- 2 tomatoes, finely chopped
- 2-3 green peppers, finely chopped
- 2 cloves garlic, minced
- 1/4 cup chopped fresh parsley
- 2 tablespoons tomato paste
- 1 teaspoon paprika
- 1/2 teaspoon ground cumin
- Salt and pepper to taste
- Olive oil for frying
- Optional: Grated cheese (such as mozzarella or feta) for topping

Instructions:

1. Preheat your oven to 180°C (350°F).
2. Wash the eggplants and pat them dry. Leaving the stems intact, slit each eggplant lengthwise, about three-quarters of the way through, creating a pocket for the stuffing. Be careful not to cut all the way through.
3. Heat some olive oil in a large skillet over medium heat. Place the eggplants in the skillet and cook them, turning occasionally, until they are lightly browned on all sides. Remove from the skillet and set aside.
4. In the same skillet, add a bit more olive oil if needed, then add the chopped onion and cook until softened and translucent.
5. Add the ground lamb or beef to the skillet and cook until browned, breaking it up with a spoon as it cooks.
6. Stir in the minced garlic, chopped tomatoes, chopped green peppers, tomato paste, paprika, cumin, salt, and pepper. Cook for a few minutes until the vegetables are softened and the mixture is well combined. Remove from heat and stir in the chopped parsley.
7. Stuff the cooked eggplants with the meat mixture, gently pressing the filling into the slits.

8. Place the stuffed eggplants in a baking dish. If desired, sprinkle some grated cheese on top.
9. Cover the baking dish with foil and bake in the preheated oven for about 30-40 minutes, or until the eggplants are tender and cooked through.
10. Once done, remove from the oven and let them cool slightly before serving.

Karnıyarık is often served with rice pilaf, bulgur pilaf, or crusty bread. Enjoy this delicious Turkish dish!

İmam Bayıldı (Stuffed eggplant with tomatoes and onions)

Ingredients:

- 4 small to medium-sized eggplants
- 2 onions, thinly sliced
- 3-4 tomatoes, thinly sliced
- 4 cloves garlic, thinly sliced
- 1/4 cup chopped fresh parsley
- 1 teaspoon ground cumin
- 1 teaspoon paprika
- Salt and pepper to taste
- Olive oil for frying and drizzling

Instructions:

1. Preheat your oven to 180°C (350°F).
2. Wash the eggplants and pat them dry. Leaving the stems intact, slit each eggplant lengthwise, creating a pocket for the stuffing. Be careful not to cut all the way through.
3. Heat some olive oil in a large skillet over medium heat. Place the eggplants in the skillet and cook them, turning occasionally, until they are lightly browned on all sides. Remove from the skillet and set aside.
4. In the same skillet, add a bit more olive oil if needed, then add the thinly sliced onions. Cook until the onions are softened and translucent.
5. Add the thinly sliced garlic to the skillet and cook for another minute until fragrant.
6. Stir in the ground cumin, paprika, salt, and pepper. Cook for another minute to toast the spices.
7. Arrange the sliced tomatoes in the skillet, covering the bottom evenly.
8. Carefully place the browned eggplants on top of the tomato-onion mixture in the skillet, with the slit sides facing upward.
9. Fill the slits of each eggplant with the cooked onion and garlic mixture. You can also place some of the mixture on top of the eggplants.
10. Sprinkle chopped parsley over the top of the stuffed eggplants.
11. Drizzle some olive oil over the stuffed eggplants.

12. Cover the skillet with a lid or aluminum foil and bake in the preheated oven for about 30-40 minutes, or until the eggplants are tender and fully cooked.
13. Once done, remove from the oven and let them cool slightly before serving.

İmam Bayıldı is often served at room temperature or slightly warm, and it pairs well with rice pilaf, bulgur pilaf, or crusty bread. Enjoy this delicious Turkish dish!

Lahmacun (Turkish pizza)

Ingredients for the dough:

- 2 cups all-purpose flour
- 1 teaspoon salt
- 1 teaspoon sugar
- 1 teaspoon dry yeast
- 3/4 cup warm water
- 2 tablespoons olive oil

Ingredients for the topping:

- 300g minced lamb or beef
- 1 onion, finely chopped
- 2 tomatoes, finely chopped
- 2 green peppers, finely chopped
- 3 cloves garlic, minced
- 2 tablespoons tomato paste
- 2 tablespoons olive oil
- 1 teaspoon paprika
- 1 teaspoon ground cumin
- Salt and pepper to taste

Instructions:

1. In a large mixing bowl, combine the flour, salt, sugar, and dry yeast. Gradually add the warm water and olive oil, mixing until a dough forms. Knead the dough for about 5-7 minutes, or until smooth and elastic. Cover the bowl with a kitchen towel and let it rise in a warm place for 1 hour.
2. While the dough is rising, prepare the topping mixture. In a skillet, heat the olive oil over medium heat. Add the minced meat and cook until browned. Add the onion, tomatoes, green peppers, and garlic. Cook until the vegetables are soft. Stir in the tomato paste, paprika, cumin, salt, and pepper. Cook for another 2-3 minutes. Set aside to cool.

3. Preheat your oven to 220°C (425°F). Divide the dough into 6-8 portions. On a floured surface, roll out each portion into a thin circle, about 1/8 inch thick.
4. Place the rolled-out dough circles onto baking sheets lined with parchment paper. Spread the meat mixture evenly over the dough, leaving a small border around the edges.
5. Bake the lahmacun in the preheated oven for 10-12 minutes, or until the edges are golden brown.
6. Remove from the oven and serve hot, garnished with fresh parsley and lemon wedges if desired.

Enjoy your homemade lahmacun!

Pide (Turkish flatbread)

Ingredients for the dough:

- 3 cups all-purpose flour
- 1 teaspoon salt
- 1 teaspoon sugar
- 1 teaspoon dry yeast
- 1 cup warm water
- 2 tablespoons olive oil

Ingredients for the topping (traditional meat filling):

- 300g ground lamb or beef
- 1 onion, finely chopped
- 2 tomatoes, diced
- 2 green peppers, finely chopped
- 2 tablespoons tomato paste
- 2 tablespoons olive oil
- 1 teaspoon paprika
- 1 teaspoon ground cumin
- Salt and pepper to taste
- Fresh parsley, chopped (for garnish)

Instructions:

1. In a large mixing bowl, combine the flour, salt, sugar, and dry yeast. Gradually add the warm water and olive oil, mixing until a dough forms. Knead the dough for about 5-7 minutes, or until it's smooth and elastic. Cover the bowl with a kitchen towel and let it rise in a warm place for 1 hour.
2. While the dough is rising, prepare the meat filling. In a skillet, heat the olive oil over medium heat. Add the ground meat and cook until browned. Add the chopped onion, diced tomatoes, and chopped green peppers. Cook until the vegetables are soft. Stir in the tomato paste, paprika, cumin, salt, and pepper. Cook for another 2-3 minutes. Set aside to cool.

3. Preheat your oven to 220°C (425°F). Divide the dough into 4 equal portions. On a floured surface, roll out each portion into an oval or boat-like shape, about 1/4 inch thick.
4. Place the rolled-out dough on baking sheets lined with parchment paper. Spoon the meat filling onto each dough boat, spreading it evenly.
5. Fold the edges of the dough slightly to form a border around the filling.
6. Bake the pide in the preheated oven for 15-20 minutes, or until the crust is golden brown and crispy.
7. Remove from the oven and sprinkle chopped fresh parsley over the top for garnish.
8. Serve the pide hot, cut into slices. Enjoy!

You can also customize the filling with your favorite ingredients, such as cheese, spinach, mushrooms, or minced chicken. Pide is delicious served with yogurt or a side salad.

Kuzu tandır (Slow-roasted lamb)

Ingredients:

- 2 kg lamb shoulder or leg, bone-in
- 4 cloves garlic, minced
- 2 tablespoons olive oil
- 2 tablespoons plain yogurt
- 1 tablespoon tomato paste
- 1 tablespoon paprika
- 1 teaspoon ground cumin
- 1 teaspoon ground coriander
- 1 teaspoon ground black pepper
- 1 teaspoon ground cinnamon
- 1 teaspoon salt, or to taste
- Juice of 1 lemon
- 1 cup water or broth (optional, for basting)

Instructions:

1. Preheat your oven to 160°C (320°F).
2. In a small bowl, mix together the minced garlic, olive oil, yogurt, tomato paste, paprika, cumin, coriander, black pepper, cinnamon, salt, and lemon juice to form a marinade.
3. Place the lamb shoulder or leg in a large roasting pan or baking dish. Using a sharp knife, make small incisions all over the meat.
4. Rub the marinade all over the lamb, making sure to massage it into the incisions. Cover the roasting pan with aluminum foil and let the lamb marinate in the refrigerator for at least 2 hours, or overnight for best results.
5. Once the lamb has marinated, remove it from the refrigerator and let it come to room temperature for about 30 minutes.
6. Place the roasting pan in the preheated oven and roast the lamb, covered with aluminum foil, for 3-4 hours, or until the meat is tender and falls off the bone easily. Baste the lamb occasionally with the pan juices or water/broth to keep it moist.

7. After the initial roasting time, remove the aluminum foil and increase the oven temperature to 200°C (400°F). Roast the lamb uncovered for an additional 30 minutes to 1 hour, or until the surface is golden brown and crispy.
8. Once done, remove the lamb from the oven and let it rest for 10-15 minutes before carving.
9. Serve the kuzu tandır hot, accompanied by rice, bulgur pilaf, roasted vegetables, or a fresh salad.

Enjoy the rich flavors and tender texture of this traditional Turkish slow-roasted lamb dish!

Etli yaprak sarma (Stuffed grape leaves with meat)

Ingredients:

- 1 jar of grape leaves (about 40-50 leaves)
- 300g ground lamb or beef
- 1 onion, finely chopped
- 1/4 cup rice, rinsed
- 2 tablespoons tomato paste
- 2 tablespoons olive oil
- 1 teaspoon ground cumin
- 1 teaspoon paprika
- 1/2 teaspoon ground cinnamon
- Salt and pepper to taste
- Juice of 1 lemon
- Water

Instructions:

1. Rinse the grape leaves under cold water to remove any brine or salt. Drain and set aside.
2. In a large mixing bowl, combine the ground meat, chopped onion, rinsed rice, tomato paste, olive oil, ground cumin, paprika, ground cinnamon, salt, and pepper. Mix well until all the ingredients are evenly incorporated.
3. Place a grape leaf flat on a clean surface, vein side up, with the stem facing you. Trim off the stem if it's too thick.
4. Take a small spoonful of the meat mixture and place it near the stem end of the grape leaf.
5. Fold the bottom of the leaf over the filling, then fold in the sides, and roll it up tightly into a cigar shape.
6. Repeat the process with the remaining grape leaves and filling mixture, arranging the stuffed grape leaves snugly in a large pot or saucepan, seam side down, in layers.
7. Once all the grape leaves are stuffed and arranged in the pot, pour enough water over them to cover them completely.
8. Place a heatproof plate or a few grape leaves on top of the stuffed grape leaves in the pot to keep them submerged during cooking.

9. Cover the pot with a lid and bring the water to a boil over medium-high heat. Once boiling, reduce the heat to low and let the stuffed grape leaves simmer gently for about 45-60 minutes, or until the rice and meat are cooked through and the grape leaves are tender.
10. Once cooked, remove the stuffed grape leaves from the heat and let them cool slightly.
11. Squeeze the juice of a lemon over the top of the stuffed grape leaves for added flavor.
12. Serve the etli yaprak sarma warm or at room temperature, garnished with lemon wedges if desired.

Enjoy this flavorful and comforting Turkish dish!

İskender kebap (Turkish doner kebab)

Ingredients:

For the döner meat:

- 500g lamb or beef, thinly sliced
- 2 tablespoons olive oil
- 2 cloves garlic, minced
- 1 teaspoon paprika
- 1 teaspoon ground cumin
- 1 teaspoon ground coriander
- Salt and pepper to taste

For the tomato sauce:

- 2 tomatoes, diced
- 1 onion, finely chopped
- 2 cloves garlic, minced
- 2 tablespoons tomato paste
- 1 tablespoon olive oil
- Salt and pepper to taste

For serving:

- Pide bread or any flatbread of your choice
- Yogurt
- Grilled peppers (optional)
- Butter (for drizzling)
- Sumac (for garnish)

Instructions:

1. Marinate the sliced lamb or beef in olive oil, minced garlic, paprika, cumin, coriander, salt, and pepper. Cover and refrigerate for at least 1 hour, or overnight for best results.
2. Preheat your grill or broiler to high heat. Grill the marinated meat slices until cooked through and nicely browned on both sides. Remove from heat and let it rest for a few minutes.
3. While the meat is resting, prepare the tomato sauce. In a skillet, heat olive oil over medium heat. Add the chopped onion and minced garlic, and cook until softened. Add the diced tomatoes and tomato paste. Cook until the tomatoes break down and the sauce thickens. Season with salt and pepper to taste.
4. Slice the pide bread into bite-sized pieces and arrange them on a serving plate.
5. Place the grilled döner meat slices over the bread pieces.
6. Spoon the tomato sauce over the meat and bread.
7. Drizzle yogurt over the tomato sauce.
8. Optionally, grill some peppers and arrange them around the plate.
9. Melt some butter and drizzle it over the İskender kebap.
10. Garnish with a sprinkle of sumac for extra flavor.
11. Serve immediately and enjoy your homemade İskender kebap!

This dish is best enjoyed fresh and hot, with the flavors of the tender meat, tangy tomato sauce, creamy yogurt, and warm bread melding together beautifully.

Kuzu şiş (Grilled lamb skewers)

Ingredients:

- 800g lamb meat (shoulder or leg), cubed
- 1 onion, grated
- 4 cloves garlic, minced
- 2 tablespoons olive oil
- 2 tablespoons plain yogurt
- 1 tablespoon tomato paste
- 1 teaspoon paprika
- 1 teaspoon ground cumin
- 1 teaspoon ground black pepper
- 1 teaspoon salt, or to taste
- Juice of 1 lemon
- Wooden or metal skewers, soaked in water if using wooden skewers
- Chopped parsley and lemon wedges for garnish (optional)

Instructions:

1. In a large mixing bowl, combine the grated onion, minced garlic, olive oil, yogurt, tomato paste, paprika, ground cumin, black pepper, salt, and lemon juice. Mix well to form a marinade.
2. Add the cubed lamb meat to the marinade and toss until the meat is evenly coated. Cover the bowl with plastic wrap and refrigerate for at least 2 hours, or overnight for best results.
3. Preheat your grill or barbecue to medium-high heat.
4. Thread the marinated lamb cubes onto the skewers, leaving a little space between each piece.
5. Brush the grill grates with oil to prevent sticking. Place the skewers on the grill and cook for about 10-12 minutes, turning occasionally, or until the lamb is cooked to your desired level of doneness and has nice grill marks on all sides.
6. Once cooked, remove the skewers from the grill and let them rest for a few minutes.
7. Garnish the kuzu şiş with chopped parsley and serve hot with lemon wedges on the side.

8. Enjoy your delicious homemade kuzu şiş with some rice, bulgur pilaf, grilled vegetables, or a fresh salad on the side.

This grilled lamb skewers recipe captures the essence of Turkish cuisine with its flavorful marinade and tender, juicy meat. It's sure to be a hit at any barbecue or dinner party!

Adana kebabı (Spicy minced meat kebabs)

Ingredients:

- 500g ground lamb or a mixture of lamb and beef
- 1 onion, grated
- 2 cloves garlic, minced
- 2 tablespoons finely chopped parsley
- 1 tablespoon tomato paste
- 1 tablespoon olive oil
- 1 tablespoon ground sumac (optional)
- 1 tablespoon ground cumin
- 1 tablespoon paprika
- 1 teaspoon red pepper flakes (adjust to taste for desired level of spiciness)
- 1 teaspoon salt, or to taste
- Freshly ground black pepper, to taste
- Wooden or metal skewers, soaked in water if using wooden skewers

Instructions:

1. In a large mixing bowl, combine the grated onion, minced garlic, finely chopped parsley, tomato paste, olive oil, ground sumac (if using), ground cumin, paprika, red pepper flakes, salt, and black pepper. Mix well to form a marinade.
2. Add the ground lamb or lamb/beef mixture to the marinade. Mix thoroughly until all the ingredients are evenly incorporated into the meat.
3. Cover the bowl with plastic wrap and refrigerate for at least 1 hour to allow the flavors to meld.
4. Preheat your grill or barbecue to medium-high heat.
5. Divide the meat mixture into portions and shape them onto skewers, pressing the meat firmly onto the skewers to form long, sausage-like shapes.
6. Brush the grill grates with oil to prevent sticking. Place the skewers on the grill and cook for about 6-8 minutes on each side, or until the kebabs are cooked through and nicely charred on the outside.
7. Once cooked, remove the Adana kebabs from the grill and let them rest for a few minutes.
8. Serve the kebabs hot with flatbread, rice, grilled vegetables, and a side of yogurt or salad.

9. Enjoy your homemade Adana kebabı with its delicious blend of spices and flavors!

This dish is perfect for outdoor grilling and is sure to impress with its bold and aromatic taste. Adjust the spiciness according to your preference, and don't forget to serve it with some fresh lemon wedges for an extra burst of flavor.

Börek (Savory pastry filled with cheese, meat, or vegetables)

Ingredients:

For the dough:

- 3 cups all-purpose flour
- 1 teaspoon salt
- 1 cup warm water
- 1/4 cup vegetable oil

For the filling:

- 250g feta cheese, crumbled
- 1 cup chopped parsley
- 1 egg, lightly beaten (optional, for brushing)

Instructions:

1. In a large mixing bowl, combine the flour and salt. Gradually add the warm water and vegetable oil, mixing until a dough forms. Knead the dough on a lightly floured surface for about 5-7 minutes, or until it becomes smooth and elastic. Cover the dough with a clean kitchen towel and let it rest for 30 minutes.
2. Preheat your oven to 180°C (350°F) and grease a baking dish with oil or butter.
3. Divide the dough into 4 equal portions. Roll out each portion into a thin sheet, about 1/8 inch thick.
4. Place one sheet of dough in the greased baking dish, making sure it covers the bottom and sides of the dish.
5. Sprinkle half of the crumbled feta cheese and half of the chopped parsley over the dough.
6. Place another sheet of dough on top of the cheese and parsley mixture, pressing down gently to adhere.
7. Repeat the layering process with the remaining cheese, parsley, and dough sheets, finishing with a layer of dough on top.
8. If desired, brush the top layer of dough with beaten egg for a shiny finish.

9. Using a sharp knife, cut the börek into squares or diamonds, being careful not to cut all the way through to the bottom layer.
10. Bake the börek in the preheated oven for 30-35 minutes, or until the top is golden brown and crispy.
11. Once done, remove the börek from the oven and let it cool slightly before serving.
12. Serve the börek warm or at room temperature, cut into squares or slices.

Enjoy your homemade börek filled with deliciously savory cheese! You can also experiment with different fillings such as spinach, ground meat, or a mixture of vegetables to create your own variations of this classic dish.

Menemen (Turkish-style scrambled eggs with tomatoes and peppers)

Ingredients:

- 4 eggs
- 2 tomatoes, diced
- 1 onion, finely chopped
- 1 green bell pepper, diced
- 1-2 tablespoons olive oil
- 1 teaspoon paprika
- 1/2 teaspoon ground cumin
- Salt and pepper to taste
- Fresh parsley, chopped (for garnish, optional)
- Feta cheese or white cheese, crumbled (optional, for serving)
- Turkish bread or crusty bread (for serving)

Instructions:

1. Heat olive oil in a large skillet over medium heat. Add the chopped onion and diced green bell pepper. Cook until softened, about 5 minutes.
2. Add the diced tomatoes to the skillet and cook until they start to break down and release their juices, about 5-7 minutes.
3. Sprinkle paprika and ground cumin over the vegetables, and season with salt and pepper to taste. Stir well to combine.
4. Crack the eggs directly into the skillet over the tomato and pepper mixture. Using a spatula, gently scramble the eggs with the vegetables until cooked to your desired consistency.
5. Once the eggs are cooked, remove the skillet from the heat.
6. Sprinkle chopped parsley over the top for garnish, if desired.
7. Serve the Menemen hot, directly from the skillet, with Turkish bread or crusty bread on the side for dipping. You can also serve it with crumbled feta cheese or white cheese for added flavor.
8. Enjoy your delicious homemade Menemen for breakfast, brunch, or any time of day!

Menemen is a versatile dish, and you can customize it according to your preferences by adding other ingredients such as garlic, chili flakes for extra heat, or different herbs like oregano or thyme. It's a flavorful and comforting dish that's sure to become a favorite in your home.

Kuru fasulye (Turkish white bean stew)

Ingredients:

- 2 cups dried white beans (such as cannellini or navy beans), soaked overnight
- 2 tablespoons olive oil
- 1 onion, finely chopped
- 2 cloves garlic, minced
- 2 tomatoes, diced
- 2 tablespoons tomato paste
- 1 teaspoon paprika
- 1 teaspoon ground cumin
- 1 teaspoon ground coriander
- 1 teaspoon dried oregano
- Salt and pepper to taste
- 4 cups water or vegetable broth
- Fresh parsley, chopped (for garnish)
- Turkish bread or rice (for serving)

Instructions:

1. Rinse the soaked white beans under cold water and drain.
2. In a large pot, heat olive oil over medium heat. Add the chopped onion and cook until softened, about 5 minutes.
3. Add the minced garlic to the pot and cook for another minute until fragrant.
4. Stir in the diced tomatoes, tomato paste, paprika, ground cumin, ground coriander, dried oregano, salt, and pepper. Cook for a few minutes until the tomatoes start to break down and release their juices.
5. Add the soaked white beans to the pot and pour in the water or vegetable broth. Stir well to combine.
6. Bring the mixture to a boil, then reduce the heat to low and let it simmer, partially covered, for about 1.5 to 2 hours, or until the beans are tender and the sauce has thickened. Stir occasionally and add more water if needed to prevent the beans from sticking to the bottom of the pot.
7. Once the beans are cooked and the sauce has thickened to your desired consistency, remove the pot from the heat.
8. Taste and adjust the seasoning if needed.

9. Serve the kuru fasulye hot, garnished with chopped fresh parsley. Serve with Turkish bread or rice on the side for a complete meal.

Enjoy this comforting and flavorful Turkish white bean stew! It's a perfect dish for colder days and is sure to warm you up with its delicious aroma and taste.

Şiş kebap (Marinated meat skewers)

Ingredients:

- 800g lamb meat (shoulder or leg), cubed
- 2 onions, grated
- 4 cloves garlic, minced
- 2 tablespoons plain yogurt
- 2 tablespoons olive oil
- Juice of 1 lemon
- 1 teaspoon paprika
- 1 teaspoon ground cumin
- 1 teaspoon ground black pepper
- 1 teaspoon salt, or to taste
- Wooden or metal skewers, soaked in water if using wooden skewers
- Chopped parsley and lemon wedges for garnish (optional)

Instructions:

1. In a large mixing bowl, combine the grated onions, minced garlic, yogurt, olive oil, lemon juice, paprika, ground cumin, black pepper, and salt. Mix well to form a marinade.
2. Add the cubed lamb meat to the marinade. Toss until all the meat is evenly coated with the marinade. Cover the bowl with plastic wrap and refrigerate for at least 2 hours, or overnight for best results.
3. Preheat your grill or barbecue to medium-high heat.
4. Thread the marinated lamb cubes onto the skewers, leaving a little space between each piece.
5. Brush the grill grates with oil to prevent sticking. Place the skewers on the grill and cook for about 8-10 minutes on each side, or until the meat is cooked through and has nice grill marks on all sides.
6. Once cooked, remove the Şiş kebap from the grill and let it rest for a few minutes.
7. Garnish with chopped parsley and serve hot with lemon wedges on the side.
8. Enjoy your homemade Şiş kebap with some rice, bulgur pilaf, grilled vegetables, or a fresh salad on the side.

This dish is perfect for outdoor grilling and is sure to impress with its juicy and flavorful meat. You can also customize the marinade according to your taste preferences by adding different herbs and spices.

Tavuk şiş (Grilled chicken skewers)

Ingredients:

- 800g boneless, skinless chicken breasts or thighs, cut into cubes
- 2 onions, grated
- 4 cloves garlic, minced
- 2 tablespoons plain yogurt
- 2 tablespoons olive oil
- Juice of 1 lemon
- 1 teaspoon paprika
- 1 teaspoon ground cumin
- 1 teaspoon ground black pepper
- 1 teaspoon salt, or to taste
- Wooden or metal skewers, soaked in water if using wooden skewers
- Chopped parsley and lemon wedges for garnish (optional)

Instructions:

1. In a large mixing bowl, combine the grated onions, minced garlic, yogurt, olive oil, lemon juice, paprika, ground cumin, black pepper, and salt. Mix well to form a marinade.
2. Add the cubed chicken pieces to the marinade. Toss until all the chicken is evenly coated with the marinade. Cover the bowl with plastic wrap and refrigerate for at least 2 hours, or overnight for best results.
3. Preheat your grill or barbecue to medium-high heat.
4. Thread the marinated chicken cubes onto the skewers, leaving a little space between each piece.
5. Brush the grill grates with oil to prevent sticking. Place the skewers on the grill and cook for about 6-8 minutes on each side, or until the chicken is cooked through and has nice grill marks on all sides.
6. Once cooked, remove the Tavuk şiş from the grill and let it rest for a few minutes.
7. Garnish with chopped parsley and serve hot with lemon wedges on the side.
8. Enjoy your homemade Tavuk şiş with some rice, bulgur pilaf, grilled vegetables, or a fresh salad on the side.

This dish is perfect for outdoor grilling and is sure to impress with its juicy and flavorful chicken. You can also customize the marinade according to your taste preferences by adding different herbs and spices.

Etli pilav (Turkish meat and rice pilaf)

Ingredients:

- 1 cup long-grain rice (such as basmati or jasmine)
- 300g lamb or beef, cubed
- 1 onion, finely chopped
- 2 tablespoons olive oil or butter
- 2 cups water or beef broth
- Salt and pepper to taste
- 1/2 teaspoon ground cumin
- 1/2 teaspoon paprika
- Pinch of saffron threads (optional, for color and flavor)
- Chopped fresh parsley or mint for garnish

Instructions:

1. Rinse the rice under cold water until the water runs clear. Drain and set aside.
2. In a large skillet or pot, heat the olive oil or butter over medium heat. Add the chopped onion and cook until softened, about 5 minutes.
3. Add the cubed lamb or beef to the skillet and cook until browned on all sides.
4. Stir in the rinsed rice and cook for a few minutes, stirring occasionally, until the rice is lightly toasted.
5. Season the mixture with salt, pepper, ground cumin, and paprika. If using saffron threads, add them to the mixture for extra color and flavor.
6. Pour in the water or beef broth, stirring to combine. Bring the mixture to a boil, then reduce the heat to low.
7. Cover the skillet or pot with a tight-fitting lid and let the pilaf simmer for about 15-20 minutes, or until the rice is cooked through and the liquid is absorbed.
8. Once the pilaf is cooked, remove it from the heat and let it rest, covered, for a few minutes.
9. Fluff the pilaf with a fork to separate the grains.
10. Transfer the etli pilav to a serving dish and garnish with chopped fresh parsley or mint.
11. Serve hot as a main course or side dish, alongside yogurt, pickles, or a salad if desired.

Enjoy your homemade etli pilav with its tender meat and fragrant rice! Adjust the seasoning according to your taste preferences, and feel free to customize the dish by adding other herbs, spices, or vegetables.

Çılbır (Poached eggs with yogurt and spicy butter)

Ingredients:

- 4 large eggs
- 1 cup plain yogurt
- 2 cloves garlic, minced
- 2 tablespoons white vinegar
- 2 tablespoons butter
- 1 teaspoon paprika
- 1/2 teaspoon ground cumin
- Salt to taste
- Fresh parsley or dill, chopped (for garnish)
- Turkish bread or crusty bread (for serving)

Instructions:

1. In a small bowl, mix the plain yogurt with the minced garlic. Season with salt to taste and set aside.
2. Fill a large skillet or wide saucepan with water and add the white vinegar. Bring the water to a gentle simmer over medium heat.
3. Crack each egg into a small bowl or ramekin. Carefully slide the eggs, one by one, into the simmering water. Cook for about 3-4 minutes for soft poached eggs or longer for firmer yolks.
4. While the eggs are poaching, melt the butter in a small saucepan over medium heat. Stir in the paprika and ground cumin, and cook for 1-2 minutes until fragrant. Remove from heat and set aside.
5. Once the eggs are cooked to your liking, use a slotted spoon to carefully remove them from the water and drain any excess water on a paper towel.
6. To serve, spoon the garlic yogurt mixture onto serving plates and spread it out into a thin layer.
7. Place the poached eggs on top of the yogurt.
8. Drizzle the spiced butter sauce over the eggs.
9. Garnish with chopped fresh parsley or dill.
10. Serve Çılbır immediately, accompanied by Turkish bread or crusty bread for dipping.

Enjoy the creamy yogurt, perfectly poached eggs, and flavorful spiced butter sauce in this delicious Turkish dish! It's perfect for a leisurely weekend breakfast or brunch.

Patlıcan kebabı (Grilled eggplant kebabs)

Ingredients:

- 2 large eggplants
- 2 tablespoons olive oil
- Salt and pepper to taste
- For the marinade:
    - 2 cloves garlic, minced
    - 2 tablespoons olive oil
    - 2 tablespoons lemon juice
    - 1 teaspoon paprika
    - 1 teaspoon ground cumin
    - 1/2 teaspoon ground coriander
    - 1/2 teaspoon chili flakes (optional, for added heat)
    - Salt and pepper to taste
- Wooden or metal skewers, soaked in water if using wooden skewers
- Chopped fresh parsley or mint for garnish (optional)
- Lemon wedges for serving

Instructions:

1. Preheat your grill or barbecue to medium-high heat.
2. Wash the eggplants and trim off the ends. Cut the eggplants into thick slices, about 1-inch thick.
3. Brush both sides of the eggplant slices with olive oil and season with salt and pepper.
4. Grill the eggplant slices on the preheated grill for about 3-4 minutes on each side, or until they are tender and lightly charred. Remove from the grill and let them cool slightly.
5. While the eggplants are grilling, prepare the marinade. In a small bowl, whisk together the minced garlic, olive oil, lemon juice, paprika, ground cumin, ground coriander, chili flakes (if using), salt, and pepper.
6. Once the eggplants have cooled slightly, thread them onto skewers.
7. Brush the marinade generously over the grilled eggplant skewers, making sure to coat them evenly.

8. Let the eggplant skewers marinate for at least 30 minutes to allow the flavors to meld.
9. Preheat the grill again to medium-high heat. Grill the marinated eggplant skewers for an additional 5-7 minutes, turning occasionally, until they are heated through and nicely caramelized.
10. Once done, remove the eggplant skewers from the grill and transfer them to a serving platter.
11. Garnish with chopped fresh parsley or mint, if desired, and serve hot with lemon wedges on the side.

Enjoy the smoky flavor and tender texture of these delicious grilled eggplant kebabs!

They make a fantastic appetizer or side dish for any barbecue or gathering.

Mercimek çorbası (Turkish lentil soup)

Ingredients:

- 1 cup red lentils, rinsed and drained
- 1 onion, finely chopped
- 1 carrot, peeled and diced
- 1 potato, peeled and diced
- 2 cloves garlic, minced
- 1 tablespoon tomato paste
- 6 cups vegetable or chicken broth
- 2 tablespoons olive oil or butter
- 1 teaspoon ground cumin
- 1 teaspoon paprika
- Salt and pepper to taste
- Juice of 1 lemon
- Fresh parsley, chopped (for garnish)
- Turkish or crusty bread (for serving)

Instructions:

1. In a large pot, heat the olive oil or butter over medium heat. Add the chopped onion and cook until softened, about 5 minutes.
2. Add the minced garlic to the pot and cook for another minute until fragrant.
3. Stir in the diced carrot and potato, and cook for a few minutes until they start to soften.
4. Add the rinsed red lentils to the pot, along with the tomato paste, ground cumin, paprika, salt, and pepper. Stir well to combine.
5. Pour in the vegetable or chicken broth and bring the mixture to a boil.
6. Once boiling, reduce the heat to low and let the soup simmer, partially covered, for about 20-25 minutes, or until the lentils and vegetables are tender.
7. Use an immersion blender or transfer a portion of the soup to a blender and blend until smooth and creamy. Be careful when blending hot liquids.
8. Return the blended soup to the pot and stir well to combine. If the soup is too thick, you can add more broth or water to reach your desired consistency.
9. Stir in the lemon juice, taste, and adjust the seasoning if needed.

10. Ladle the mercimek çorbası into serving bowls and garnish with chopped fresh parsley.
11. Serve hot with Turkish or crusty bread on the side for dipping.

Enjoy the warm and comforting flavors of this Turkish lentil soup! It's perfect for chilly days and makes a satisfying meal on its own or as a starter for any dinner.

Hünkar beğendi (Lamb stew served over creamy eggplant puree)

Ingredients:

For the lamb stew:

- 800g lamb shoulder or leg, cut into cubes
- 2 tablespoons olive oil
- 1 onion, finely chopped
- 2 cloves garlic, minced
- 2 tomatoes, diced
- 2 tablespoons tomato paste
- 1 teaspoon paprika
- 1 teaspoon ground cumin
- 1 teaspoon ground cinnamon
- Salt and pepper to taste
- 2 cups beef or vegetable broth
- Fresh parsley, chopped (for garnish)

For the eggplant puree (beğendi):

- 2 large eggplants
- 2 tablespoons butter
- 2 tablespoons all-purpose flour
- 2 cups milk
- 1 cup grated cheese (such as kasar or mozzarella)
- Salt and pepper to taste
- Pinch of nutmeg (optional)

Instructions:

1. Start by preparing the lamb stew. In a large pot or Dutch oven, heat the olive oil over medium heat. Add the chopped onion and cook until softened, about 5 minutes.
2. Add the minced garlic to the pot and cook for another minute until fragrant.
3. Add the cubed lamb to the pot and cook until browned on all sides.

4. Stir in the diced tomatoes, tomato paste, paprika, ground cumin, ground cinnamon, salt, and pepper. Cook for a few minutes until the tomatoes start to break down.
5. Pour in the beef or vegetable broth, stirring to combine. Bring the mixture to a boil, then reduce the heat to low and let it simmer, covered, for about 1.5 to 2 hours, or until the lamb is tender and the sauce has thickened.
6. While the lamb stew is simmering, prepare the eggplant puree (beğendi). Preheat your oven to 200°C (400°F).
7. Prick the eggplants with a fork and place them on a baking sheet. Roast in the preheated oven for about 45-50 minutes, or until the eggplants are soft and collapsed.
8. Remove the eggplants from the oven and let them cool slightly. Peel off the skins and discard.
9. In a separate saucepan, melt the butter over medium heat. Stir in the flour and cook for 1-2 minutes until lightly golden.
10. Gradually pour in the milk, whisking constantly to prevent lumps from forming. Cook until the mixture thickens and coats the back of a spoon.
11. Add the roasted eggplant flesh to the milk mixture and mash it with a fork or potato masher until smooth.
12. Stir in the grated cheese until melted and well combined. Season with salt, pepper, and nutmeg (if using).
13. To serve, spoon the creamy eggplant puree onto serving plates. Top with the lamb stew and garnish with chopped fresh parsley.
14. Serve hünkar beğendi hot, accompanied by rice or crusty bread.

Enjoy the rich and flavorful combination of tender lamb stew and creamy eggplant puree in this classic Turkish dish! It's sure to impress with its delicious taste and elegant presentation.

Balık köfte (Fish meatballs)

Ingredients:

- 500g white fish fillets (such as cod, haddock, or tilapia), skin removed and bones removed
- 1 onion, finely chopped
- 2 cloves garlic, minced
- 1/4 cup fresh parsley, chopped
- 1/4 cup fresh dill, chopped
- 1 teaspoon ground cumin
- 1 teaspoon paprika
- 1/2 teaspoon ground coriander
- 1/2 teaspoon chili flakes (optional, for added heat)
- 1 egg
- 1/4 cup breadcrumbs
- Salt and pepper to taste
- Olive oil for frying
- Lemon wedges for serving

Instructions:

1. Pat the fish fillets dry with paper towels and cut them into chunks. Place the fish chunks in a food processor and pulse until finely ground.
2. Transfer the ground fish to a large mixing bowl. Add the finely chopped onion, minced garlic, chopped parsley, chopped dill, ground cumin, paprika, ground coriander, chili flakes (if using), egg, breadcrumbs, salt, and pepper to taste.
3. Mix all the ingredients together until well combined. The mixture should hold together easily when shaped into balls. If it's too wet, you can add more breadcrumbs as needed.
4. Use your hands to shape the fish mixture into small balls, about the size of golf balls. Place the fish balls on a plate or tray lined with parchment paper.
5. Heat some olive oil in a large skillet or frying pan over medium heat. Add the fish balls to the pan in batches, making sure not to overcrowd the pan.
6. Cook the fish balls for about 3-4 minutes on each side, or until golden brown and cooked through. Use a spatula to gently flip them halfway through cooking.

7. Once cooked, transfer the fish balls to a plate lined with paper towels to drain any excess oil.
8. Serve the balık köfte hot, with lemon wedges on the side for squeezing over the top.

Enjoy your homemade balık köfte as a delicious appetizer or main dish! They're crispy on the outside, tender on the inside, and bursting with flavor from the herbs and spices.

Kuzu tandır pilavı (Rice pilaf with lamb)

Ingredients:

For the lamb:

- 800g lamb shoulder or leg, cut into large chunks
- 2 onions, sliced
- 4 cloves garlic, minced
- 2 tablespoons tomato paste
- 1 tablespoon olive oil
- 1 teaspoon ground cumin
- 1 teaspoon ground coriander
- 1 teaspoon paprika
- 1/2 teaspoon ground cinnamon
- Salt and pepper to taste
- 1 cup water or beef broth

For the rice pilaf:

- 1 cup basmati rice, rinsed and drained
- 1 3/4 cups water or chicken broth
- 2 tablespoons butter or olive oil
- 1 onion, finely chopped
- 2 cloves garlic, minced
- Salt and pepper to taste
- Chopped fresh parsley or mint for garnish (optional)

Instructions:

1. Preheat your oven to 160°C (325°F).
2. In a large roasting pan or Dutch oven, combine the lamb chunks, sliced onions, minced garlic, tomato paste, olive oil, ground cumin, ground coriander, paprika, ground cinnamon, salt, pepper, and water or beef broth. Mix well to coat the lamb evenly with the spices and other ingredients.

3. Cover the roasting pan or Dutch oven with a lid or aluminum foil. Place it in the preheated oven and bake for about 2.5 to 3 hours, or until the lamb is tender and falling apart.
4. While the lamb is cooking, prepare the rice pilaf. In a saucepan, heat the butter or olive oil over medium heat. Add the chopped onion and cook until softened, about 5 minutes.
5. Add the minced garlic to the saucepan and cook for another minute until fragrant.
6. Stir in the rinsed basmati rice and cook for a few minutes, stirring frequently, until lightly toasted.
7. Pour in the water or chicken broth, season with salt and pepper to taste, and bring the mixture to a boil.
8. Once boiling, reduce the heat to low, cover the saucepan with a lid, and let the rice simmer for about 15-20 minutes, or until the liquid is absorbed and the rice is cooked through.
9. Once the lamb is done cooking, remove it from the oven and shred the meat using two forks.
10. Serve the tender lamb over the cooked rice pilaf, garnished with chopped fresh parsley or mint if desired.
11. Enjoy your delicious kuzu tandır pilavı, a flavorful and comforting Turkish dish that's perfect for sharing with family and friends.

Kuzu güveç (Lamb stew cooked in a clay pot)

Ingredients:

- 800g lamb shoulder or leg, cut into chunks
- 2 onions, chopped
- 3 cloves garlic, minced
- 2 tomatoes, diced
- 2 tablespoons tomato paste
- 2 tablespoons olive oil
- 1 teaspoon paprika
- 1 teaspoon ground cumin
- 1/2 teaspoon ground cinnamon
- Salt and pepper to taste
- 1 cup water or beef broth
- 2 potatoes, peeled and cut into chunks
- 2 carrots, peeled and sliced
- 1 red bell pepper, sliced
- Fresh parsley or dill, chopped (for garnish)
- Turkish bread or crusty bread (for serving)

Instructions:

1. Preheat your oven to 180°C (350°F).
2. In a large bowl, combine the lamb chunks, chopped onions, minced garlic, diced tomatoes, tomato paste, olive oil, paprika, ground cumin, ground cinnamon, salt, and pepper. Mix well to coat the lamb evenly with the spices and other ingredients.
3. Transfer the lamb mixture to a clay pot or ovenproof casserole dish.
4. Add the water or beef broth to the pot, stirring to combine.
5. Arrange the potato chunks, carrot slices, and red bell pepper slices over the lamb mixture in the pot.
6. Cover the pot with a lid or aluminum foil.
7. Place the pot in the preheated oven and bake for about 2 to 2.5 hours, or until the lamb is tender and the vegetables are cooked through.
8. Once the kuzu güveç is done cooking, remove it from the oven and garnish with chopped fresh parsley or dill.

9. Serve the lamb stew hot, directly from the clay pot, with Turkish bread or crusty bread on the side for dipping.
10. Enjoy your homemade kuzu güveç, a comforting and delicious Turkish dish that's perfect for sharing with family and friends.

Tavuk sarma (Stuffed chicken rolls)

Ingredients:

For the chicken rolls:

- 4 boneless, skinless chicken breasts
- Salt and pepper to taste
- 1 tablespoon olive oil

For the filling:

- 1 cup cooked rice (white or brown)
- 1 onion, finely chopped
- 2 cloves garlic, minced
- 1/2 cup cooked chickpeas, mashed
- 1/4 cup chopped fresh parsley
- 1/4 cup chopped fresh dill
- 1/4 cup chopped fresh mint
- 1/4 cup pine nuts or chopped walnuts
- 1 teaspoon ground cumin
- 1 teaspoon paprika
- Salt and pepper to taste
- Juice of 1 lemon

For the sauce:

- 1 cup chicken broth
- 2 tablespoons tomato paste
- 1 tablespoon olive oil
- 1 teaspoon paprika
- Salt and pepper to taste

Instructions:

1. Preheat your oven to 180°C (350°F).

2. Place each chicken breast between two sheets of plastic wrap or parchment paper. Use a meat mallet or rolling pin to pound the chicken breasts until they are about 1/4 inch thick. Season each chicken breast with salt and pepper on both sides.
3. In a large mixing bowl, prepare the filling by combining the cooked rice, chopped onion, minced garlic, mashed chickpeas, chopped parsley, chopped dill, chopped mint, pine nuts or chopped walnuts, ground cumin, paprika, salt, pepper, and lemon juice. Mix well to combine.
4. Spoon the filling mixture onto each chicken breast, dividing it evenly among them. Spread the filling in an even layer, leaving a small border around the edges.
5. Roll up each chicken breast tightly to enclose the filling, securing with toothpicks if needed.
6. Heat olive oil in a large skillet over medium-high heat. Add the stuffed chicken rolls to the skillet and cook for about 2-3 minutes on each side, or until lightly browned.
7. While the chicken rolls are browning, prepare the sauce. In a small bowl, whisk together the chicken broth, tomato paste, olive oil, paprika, salt, and pepper.
8. Transfer the browned chicken rolls to a baking dish. Pour the sauce over the chicken rolls.
9. Cover the baking dish with aluminum foil and bake in the preheated oven for about 25-30 minutes, or until the chicken is cooked through and the sauce is bubbling.
10. Once done, remove the toothpicks from the chicken rolls.
11. Serve the tavuk sarma hot, garnished with additional chopped fresh herbs if desired.

Enjoy your flavorful and tender tavuk sarma with a side of rice, bulgur pilaf, or a fresh salad! It's a perfect dish for a special occasion or family dinner.

Zeytinyağlı yaprak sarma (Stuffed grape leaves with rice)

Ingredients:

- 1 jar of grape leaves in brine (about 60-70 leaves), or fresh grape leaves if available
- 1 cup rice (short or medium-grain)
- 1 onion, finely chopped
- 2 tablespoons pine nuts or chopped walnuts (optional)
- 2 tablespoons currants or raisins (optional)
- 1/4 cup chopped fresh parsley
- 1/4 cup chopped fresh dill
- 1/4 cup chopped fresh mint
- 1/4 cup olive oil, plus more for drizzling
- Juice of 1 lemon
- Salt and pepper to taste
- Water
- Greek yogurt (for serving, optional)
- Lemon wedges (for serving, optional)

Instructions:

1. If you're using grape leaves from a jar, remove them from the brine and rinse them thoroughly under cold water to remove excess salt. If you're using fresh grape leaves, blanch them in boiling water for a few seconds, then rinse them under cold water and pat dry with paper towels.
2. In a large mixing bowl, combine the rice, chopped onion, pine nuts or chopped walnuts (if using), currants or raisins (if using), chopped parsley, chopped dill, chopped mint, olive oil, lemon juice, salt, and pepper. Mix well to combine.
3. Place a grape leaf on a flat surface, shiny side down and vein side up. Place about a tablespoon of the rice mixture near the stem end of the leaf.
4. Fold the bottom of the leaf over the filling, then fold in the sides, and roll it up tightly into a cylinder shape. Repeat with the remaining grape leaves and rice mixture.
5. Line the bottom of a large pot with any torn or extra grape leaves. Place the stuffed grape leaves seam side down in the pot, packing them tightly together in a single layer.

6. Drizzle some olive oil over the stuffed grape leaves in the pot. Place a heatproof plate upside down over the grape leaves to keep them from unraveling during cooking.
7. Pour enough water into the pot to just cover the stuffed grape leaves.
8. Cover the pot with a lid and bring the water to a boil over medium-high heat. Once boiling, reduce the heat to low and let the stuffed grape leaves simmer gently for about 30-40 minutes, or until the rice is cooked and tender.
9. Once done, remove the pot from the heat and let the stuffed grape leaves cool slightly in the pot.
10. Serve the zeytinyağlı yaprak sarma warm or at room temperature, drizzled with some extra olive oil and accompanied by Greek yogurt and lemon wedges if desired.

Enjoy the delicious flavors of these stuffed grape leaves with rice, a classic dish that's perfect for sharing with family and friends!

Karışık kızartma (Mixed fried vegetables)

Ingredients:

- Assorted vegetables, such as eggplant, zucchini, bell peppers, cauliflower, and carrots
- All-purpose flour
- Cornstarch
- Baking powder
- Salt and pepper to taste
- Water
- Vegetable oil for frying
- Lemon wedges for serving
- Optional: yogurt or garlic yogurt sauce for dipping

Instructions:

1. Wash and prepare the vegetables. Peel if necessary, and cut them into bite-sized pieces or slices. Pat them dry with paper towels to remove excess moisture.
2. In a mixing bowl, prepare the batter by combining equal parts all-purpose flour and cornstarch. Add a pinch of baking powder, salt, and pepper to taste. Gradually whisk in water until you have a smooth, thick batter.
3. Heat vegetable oil in a deep fryer or large skillet over medium-high heat until it reaches 180°C (350°F).
4. Dip the vegetable pieces into the batter, coating them evenly. Shake off any excess batter.
5. Carefully place the battered vegetables into the hot oil, making sure not to overcrowd the pan. Fry in batches if necessary to ensure even cooking.
6. Fry the vegetables for 3-5 minutes, or until they are crispy and golden brown. Use a slotted spoon to remove them from the oil and transfer them to a plate lined with paper towels to drain excess oil.
7. Repeat the frying process with the remaining vegetables.
8. Once all the vegetables are fried, arrange them on a serving platter. Serve hot with lemon wedges on the side for squeezing over the top.
9. Optionally, serve karışık kızartma with yogurt or garlic yogurt sauce for dipping.
10. Enjoy your homemade karışık kızartma as a delicious appetizer or side dish, perfect for sharing with family and friends!

Feel free to customize the vegetables used in this dish according to your preferences and what's in season. You can also experiment with different spices and herbs to flavor the batter.

Şakşuka (Turkish vegetable stew)

Ingredients:

- 2 eggplants, peeled and cubed
- 2 zucchinis, cubed
- 2 bell peppers (any color), seeded and sliced
- 2 onions, thinly sliced
- 4 tomatoes, diced
- 4 cloves garlic, minced
- 3 tablespoons tomato paste
- 2 tablespoons olive oil
- 1 teaspoon paprika
- 1 teaspoon ground cumin
- 1/2 teaspoon chili flakes (optional, for heat)
- Salt and pepper to taste
- Fresh parsley or cilantro, chopped (for garnish)
- Greek yogurt or crusty bread (for serving)

Instructions:

1. Heat the olive oil in a large skillet or pot over medium heat. Add the sliced onions and minced garlic, and sauté until softened and fragrant, about 5 minutes.
2. Add the cubed eggplants and zucchinis to the skillet. Cook, stirring occasionally, until they start to soften, about 5-7 minutes.
3. Stir in the sliced bell peppers and diced tomatoes. Cook for another 5 minutes, until the vegetables are tender but still slightly crisp.
4. Add the tomato paste, paprika, ground cumin, chili flakes (if using), salt, and pepper to the skillet. Stir well to combine, making sure the vegetables are coated in the spices and tomato paste.
5. Reduce the heat to low, cover the skillet, and let the şakşuka simmer for about 15-20 minutes, stirring occasionally, until the vegetables are fully cooked and the flavors have melded together.
6. Once done, taste and adjust the seasoning if needed.
7. Transfer the şakşuka to a serving dish and garnish with chopped fresh parsley or cilantro.

8. Serve hot or at room temperature, with a dollop of Greek yogurt on top if desired, and crusty bread on the side for dipping.

Enjoy the rich flavors and vibrant colors of this delicious Turkish vegetable stew! It's perfect as a main course or side dish, and it's sure to be a hit at any meal.

Közlenmiş biber salatası (Roasted pepper salad)

Ingredients:

- 4 large bell peppers (red, yellow, or a combination)
- 2 tablespoons olive oil
- 2 cloves garlic, minced
- 1 tablespoon lemon juice
- 1 teaspoon ground cumin
- 1/2 teaspoon paprika
- Salt and pepper to taste
- Chopped fresh parsley or cilantro (for garnish)
- Optional: crumbled feta cheese or chopped olives for added flavor

Instructions:

1. Preheat your grill to medium-high heat or preheat your oven to broil.
2. Wash the bell peppers and pat them dry with paper towels. Place the whole bell peppers on the grill or on a baking sheet lined with aluminum foil.
3. Roast the bell peppers, turning occasionally, until the skin is charred and blistered on all sides. This usually takes about 10-15 minutes on the grill or 15-20 minutes under the broiler in the oven.
4. Once the bell peppers are charred, remove them from the heat and transfer them to a bowl. Cover the bowl with plastic wrap or a kitchen towel and let the bell peppers steam for about 10 minutes. This will help loosen the skin, making it easier to peel.
5. After steaming, carefully peel off the charred skin from the bell peppers. Remove the stem and seeds, and slice the peppers into thin strips.
6. In a large bowl, whisk together the olive oil, minced garlic, lemon juice, ground cumin, paprika, salt, and pepper to make the dressing.
7. Add the sliced roasted bell peppers to the bowl with the dressing. Toss gently to coat the peppers evenly with the dressing.
8. Let the közlenmiş biber salatası marinate in the refrigerator for at least 30 minutes to allow the flavors to meld together.
9. Before serving, garnish the salad with chopped fresh parsley or cilantro. You can also add crumbled feta cheese or chopped olives for extra flavor if desired.

10. Serve közlenmiş biber salatası chilled or at room temperature as a delicious and colorful side dish or appetizer.

Enjoy the smoky and tangy flavors of this roasted pepper salad, perfect for summer gatherings or as a refreshing addition to any meal!

Patlıcan salatası (Eggplant salad)

Ingredients:

- 2 large eggplants
- 2 cloves garlic, minced
- 2 tablespoons lemon juice
- 2 tablespoons olive oil
- Salt and pepper to taste
- 2 tablespoons chopped fresh parsley
- 1 tablespoon chopped fresh mint (optional)
- Sumac or paprika for garnish (optional)
- Greek yogurt or tahini (optional, for serving)
- Crusty bread or pita chips (for serving)

Instructions:

1. Preheat your grill to medium-high heat or preheat your oven to 200°C (400°F) for roasting.
2. Wash the eggplants and pat them dry with paper towels. Pierce the eggplants in several places with a fork to prevent them from bursting during cooking.
3. If grilling: Place the whole eggplants directly on the grill grates. Grill, turning occasionally, until the skin is charred and the flesh is soft, about 15-20 minutes. If roasting: Place the eggplants on a baking sheet lined with aluminum foil. Roast in the preheated oven for about 40-45 minutes, or until the skin is charred and the flesh is soft.
4. Once the eggplants are cooked, remove them from the heat and let them cool slightly.
5. Peel off the charred skin from the eggplants and discard. Place the peeled eggplant flesh in a colander or strainer to drain excess liquid for about 10-15 minutes.
6. Transfer the drained eggplant flesh to a cutting board and chop it finely with a knife.
7. In a large bowl, combine the chopped eggplant with minced garlic, lemon juice, olive oil, salt, pepper, chopped parsley, and chopped mint (if using). Mix well to combine.
8. Taste and adjust the seasoning if needed.

9. Transfer the patlıcan salatası to a serving dish. Sprinkle sumac or paprika on top for garnish, if desired.
10. Serve patlıcan salatası at room temperature or chilled, with a dollop of Greek yogurt or tahini on top if desired, and crusty bread or pita chips on the side for dipping.

Enjoy the creamy texture and rich flavor of this delicious Turkish eggplant salad, perfect as an appetizer or side dish for any occasion!

Haydari (Yogurt dip with garlic and herbs)

Ingredients:

- 1 cup Greek yogurt
- 2 cloves garlic, minced
- 2 tablespoons fresh dill, finely chopped
- 2 tablespoons fresh mint, finely chopped
- 1 tablespoon fresh parsley, finely chopped
- 1 tablespoon extra virgin olive oil
- 1/2 teaspoon ground cumin
- Salt and pepper to taste
- Optional: red pepper flakes or paprika for garnish
- Optional: lemon wedges for serving

Instructions:

1. In a mixing bowl, combine the Greek yogurt, minced garlic, chopped dill, chopped mint, chopped parsley, extra virgin olive oil, and ground cumin. Mix well to combine.
2. Season the haydari with salt and pepper to taste. Adjust the seasoning according to your preference.
3. Transfer the haydari to a serving dish. Drizzle a little extra olive oil on top and sprinkle with red pepper flakes or paprika for garnish, if desired.
4. Serve the haydari chilled or at room temperature, with lemon wedges on the side if you like.
5. Enjoy the creamy and flavorful haydari with pita bread, crusty bread, or vegetable sticks for dipping.

This refreshing and tangy yogurt dip is perfect for parties, gatherings, or as a delicious addition to any meal. It's simple to make and bursting with fresh herbs and garlic flavor.

Cacık (Turkish yogurt and cucumber dip)

Ingredients:

- 1 cup Greek yogurt
- 1/2 cucumber, grated and squeezed to remove excess moisture
- 1-2 cloves garlic, minced
- 1 tablespoon fresh dill, finely chopped
- 1 tablespoon fresh mint, finely chopped
- 1 tablespoon extra virgin olive oil
- 1 teaspoon lemon juice (optional)
- Salt to taste
- Optional: pinch of paprika or red pepper flakes for garnish

Instructions:

1. In a mixing bowl, combine the Greek yogurt, grated cucumber, minced garlic, chopped dill, chopped mint, extra virgin olive oil, and lemon juice (if using). Mix well to combine.
2. Season the cacık with salt to taste. Adjust the seasoning according to your preference.
3. Transfer the cacık to a serving dish. Drizzle a little extra olive oil on top and sprinkle with a pinch of paprika or red pepper flakes for garnish, if desired.
4. Serve the cacık chilled, as a dip or side dish.
5. Enjoy the creamy and cooling flavors of this traditional Turkish yogurt and cucumber dip with pita bread, crackers, or vegetable sticks.

Cacık is a versatile dish that pairs well with grilled meats, kebabs, or as a refreshing accompaniment to spicy dishes. It's also a great way to incorporate fresh herbs and vegetables into your diet while keeping things light and healthy.

Hummus (Chickpea dip)

Ingredients:

- 1 can (15 ounces) chickpeas (garbanzo beans), drained and rinsed
- 1/4 cup tahini
- 2 cloves garlic, minced
- 2 tablespoons lemon juice
- 2 tablespoons extra virgin olive oil, plus more for serving
- 1/2 teaspoon ground cumin
- Salt to taste
- Water (as needed for consistency)
- Optional toppings: paprika, chopped fresh parsley, pine nuts, or olives

Instructions:

1. In a food processor, combine the drained chickpeas, tahini, minced garlic, lemon juice, olive oil, ground cumin, and a pinch of salt.
2. Process the mixture until smooth and creamy, scraping down the sides of the food processor as needed. If the hummus is too thick, add water, 1 tablespoon at a time, until you reach your desired consistency.
3. Taste the hummus and adjust the seasoning, adding more salt or lemon juice if needed.
4. Transfer the hummus to a serving bowl. Drizzle with a little extra olive oil and sprinkle with your choice of toppings, such as paprika, chopped fresh parsley, pine nuts, or olives.
5. Serve the hummus with pita bread, crackers, or vegetable sticks for dipping.
6. Enjoy the creamy and flavorful homemade hummus as a delicious appetizer, snack, or spread!

Hummus is a versatile dish that can be customized to suit your taste preferences. Feel free to experiment with additional ingredients like roasted red peppers, sun-dried tomatoes, or fresh herbs to create your own unique variations.

Tarama (Fish roe dip)

Ingredients:

- 100g fish roe (tarama), soaked in water for 30 minutes and drained
- 1 small onion, finely grated or minced
- 1/2 cup breadcrumbs (preferably white bread without crusts)
- 1/4 cup extra virgin olive oil, plus more for serving
- 2 tablespoons lemon juice
- Salt and pepper to taste
- Optional garnishes: chopped fresh parsley, olives, capers, or red onion slices

Instructions:

1. Place the soaked and drained fish roe in a food processor or blender. Add the grated or minced onion, breadcrumbs, olive oil, and lemon juice.
2. Blend the mixture until smooth and creamy, scraping down the sides of the food processor or blender as needed.
3. Taste the tarama and season with salt and pepper to taste. Blend again to incorporate the seasoning.
4. Transfer the tarama to a serving bowl. Drizzle with a little extra olive oil and garnish with your choice of toppings, such as chopped fresh parsley, olives, capers, or red onion slices.
5. Serve the tarama with pita bread, crackers, or vegetable sticks for dipping.
6. Enjoy the creamy and flavorful homemade tarama as a delicious appetizer or spread!

Tarama is best served fresh but can be stored in an airtight container in the refrigerator for up to 3 days. Before serving leftovers, give it a quick stir and adjust the seasoning if necessary.

Ezme (Spicy tomato and pepper relish)

Ingredients:

- 3 medium tomatoes, finely chopped
- 2-3 hot green peppers (such as serrano or jalapeño), finely chopped
- 1/2 red bell pepper, finely chopped
- 1 small onion, finely chopped
- 2 cloves garlic, minced
- 2 tablespoons tomato paste
- 2 tablespoons extra virgin olive oil
- 2 tablespoons lemon juice
- 1 teaspoon ground cumin
- 1 teaspoon paprika
- 1/2 teaspoon red pepper flakes (adjust to taste)
- Salt and pepper to taste
- Chopped fresh parsley or mint for garnish (optional)

Instructions:

1. In a mixing bowl, combine the finely chopped tomatoes, hot green peppers, red bell pepper, onion, and minced garlic.
2. Add the tomato paste, extra virgin olive oil, lemon juice, ground cumin, paprika, red pepper flakes, salt, and pepper to the bowl. Mix well to combine, ensuring that the ingredients are evenly distributed.
3. Taste the ezme and adjust the seasoning as needed, adding more salt, pepper, or lemon juice according to your preference.
4. Cover the bowl with plastic wrap and refrigerate the ezme for at least 1 hour to allow the flavors to meld together.
5. Before serving, give the ezme a final stir and transfer it to a serving dish. Garnish with chopped fresh parsley or mint if desired.
6. Serve the ezme with crusty bread, pita chips, or as a condiment alongside grilled meats.
7. Enjoy the bold flavors and spicy kick of this delicious Turkish tomato and pepper relish!

Feel free to adjust the spiciness of the ezme by adding more or fewer hot peppers and red pepper flakes according to your taste preferences. You can also customize the recipe by adding other ingredients like chopped cucumber or herbs for added freshness.

Acılı ezme (Spicy tomato and pepper dip)

Ingredients:

- 4 medium tomatoes, finely chopped
- 2-3 hot green peppers (such as serrano or jalapeño), finely chopped
- 1/2 red onion, finely chopped
- 2 cloves garlic, minced
- 2 tablespoons tomato paste
- 2 tablespoons extra virgin olive oil
- 2 tablespoons lemon juice
- 1 teaspoon ground cumin
- 1 teaspoon paprika
- 1/2 teaspoon red pepper flakes (adjust to taste)
- Salt and pepper to taste
- Chopped fresh parsley or mint for garnish (optional)

Instructions:

1. In a mixing bowl, combine the finely chopped tomatoes, hot green peppers, red onion, and minced garlic.
2. Add the tomato paste, extra virgin olive oil, lemon juice, ground cumin, paprika, red pepper flakes, salt, and pepper to the bowl. Mix well to combine, ensuring that the ingredients are evenly distributed.
3. Taste the acılı ezme and adjust the seasoning as needed, adding more salt, pepper, or lemon juice according to your preference.
4. Cover the bowl with plastic wrap and refrigerate the acılı ezme for at least 1 hour to allow the flavors to meld together.
5. Before serving, give the acılı ezme a final stir and transfer it to a serving dish. Garnish with chopped fresh parsley or mint if desired.
6. Serve the acılı ezme with crusty bread, pita chips, or as a condiment alongside grilled meats.
7. Enjoy the bold flavors and spicy kick of this delicious Turkish tomato and pepper dip!

Feel free to adjust the spiciness of the acılı ezme by adding more or fewer hot peppers and red pepper flakes according to your taste preferences. You can also customize the recipe by adding other ingredients like chopped cucumber or herbs for added freshness.

Patlıcan ezmesi (Eggplant dip)

Ingredients:

- 2 medium eggplants
- 2 cloves garlic, minced
- 2 tablespoons lemon juice
- 2 tablespoons extra virgin olive oil
- 1 tablespoon tahini (sesame paste)
- 1 teaspoon ground cumin
- Salt and pepper to taste
- Chopped fresh parsley for garnish
- Optional: red pepper flakes or paprika for garnish

Instructions:

1. Preheat your grill to medium-high heat or preheat your oven to 200°C (400°F) for roasting.
2. Wash the eggplants and pat them dry with paper towels. Pierce the eggplants in several places with a fork to prevent them from bursting during cooking.
3. If grilling: Place the whole eggplants directly on the grill grates. Grill, turning occasionally, until the skin is charred and the flesh is soft, about 15-20 minutes. If roasting: Place the eggplants on a baking sheet lined with aluminum foil. Roast in the preheated oven for about 40-45 minutes, or until the skin is charred and the flesh is soft.
4. Once the eggplants are cooked, remove them from the heat and let them cool slightly.
5. Peel off the charred skin from the eggplants and discard. Place the peeled eggplant flesh in a colander or strainer to drain excess liquid for about 10-15 minutes.
6. Transfer the drained eggplant flesh to a cutting board and chop it finely with a knife.
7. In a mixing bowl, combine the chopped eggplant with minced garlic, lemon juice, extra virgin olive oil, tahini, ground cumin, salt, and pepper. Mix well to combine.
8. Taste the patlıcan ezmesi and adjust the seasoning as needed, adding more salt, pepper, or lemon juice according to your preference.

9. Transfer the patlıcan ezmesi to a serving dish. Drizzle with a little extra olive oil and garnish with chopped fresh parsley and a sprinkle of red pepper flakes or paprika if desired.
10. Serve the patlıcan ezmesi with crusty bread, pita chips, or vegetable sticks for dipping.
11. Enjoy the creamy and flavorful homemade eggplant dip as a delicious appetizer or spread!

Feel free to customize the patlıcan ezmesi by adding other ingredients like roasted red peppers, roasted garlic, or chopped herbs for added flavor.

Mücver (Zucchini fritters)

Ingredients:

- 2 medium zucchinis
- 1 small onion, grated
- 2 cloves garlic, minced
- 1/4 cup chopped fresh parsley
- 1/4 cup chopped fresh dill
- 2 eggs, lightly beaten
- 1/2 cup all-purpose flour
- 1 teaspoon baking powder
- 1 teaspoon salt
- 1/2 teaspoon black pepper
- Vegetable oil for frying
- Greek yogurt or tzatziki sauce for serving (optional)

Instructions:

1. Grate the zucchinis using a box grater or food processor. Place the grated zucchini in a colander set over a bowl and sprinkle with salt. Let it sit for about 10-15 minutes to release excess moisture.
2. While the zucchini is draining, prepare the remaining ingredients. In a large mixing bowl, combine the grated onion, minced garlic, chopped parsley, chopped dill, beaten eggs, flour, baking powder, salt, and black pepper. Mix well to combine.
3. Squeeze the grated zucchini with your hands or a clean kitchen towel to remove as much moisture as possible. Add the squeezed zucchini to the mixing bowl with the other ingredients and mix until everything is well combined.
4. Heat vegetable oil in a large skillet over medium heat. Once the oil is hot, drop spoonfuls of the mücver batter into the skillet, flattening them slightly with the back of the spoon.
5. Fry the mücver in batches, making sure not to overcrowd the skillet, until golden brown and crispy on both sides, about 3-4 minutes per side. Use a spatula to flip them halfway through cooking.
6. Once cooked, transfer the mücver to a plate lined with paper towels to drain excess oil.

7. Repeat the frying process with the remaining batter until all the mücver is cooked.
8. Serve the mücver hot as an appetizer, side dish, or light meal, accompanied by Greek yogurt or tzatziki sauce for dipping if desired.
9. Enjoy the crispy and flavorful mücver with its fresh herb and zucchini taste!

Feel free to customize your mücver by adding other ingredients like crumbled feta cheese, chopped scallions, or grated carrots for extra flavor and texture.

Sigara böreği (Rolled phyllo pastry filled with cheese or herbs)

Ingredients:

- Phyllo pastry sheets or ready-made dough sheets
- White cheese or feta cheese (you can also use mozzarella or ricotta cheese)
- Finely chopped parsley or dill
- 1 Egg
- Vegetable oil or melted butter (for brushing the pastry sheets)
- Sesame seeds or nigella seeds (for garnish)

Preparation:

1. If you're using phyllo pastry sheets, lay them out on a clean surface.
2. Sprinkle the wide part of the pastry sheet with cheese and finely chopped parsley or dill. Optionally, you can add spices or herbs of your choice.
3. Roll up the pastry sheet tightly starting from the wide end. Seal the roll tightly with your fingers.
4. Cut the rolled pastry into cigar-shaped pieces using a knife.
5. Beat the egg in a bowl. Dip each piece of sigara böreği into the beaten egg, then coat it with sesame seeds or nigella seeds.
6. Repeat the process until all the sigara böreği pieces are prepared.
7. Place all the sigara böreği pieces on a baking sheet lined with parchment paper.
8. Bake in a preheated oven at 180 degrees Celsius (350 degrees Fahrenheit) until the tops are golden brown, usually for about 20-25 minutes.
9. Remove from the oven and serve hot. You can serve them with yogurt or spicy sauce if desired.

Enjoy your homemade sigara böreği!

Kabak mücveri (Zucchini pancakes)

Ingredients:

- 2 medium-sized zucchinis
- 1 small onion
- 2 cloves of garlic (optional)
- 1/2 cup of crumbled feta cheese (optional)
- 1/4 cup of chopped fresh parsley or dill
- 2 eggs
- 1/2 cup of all-purpose flour
- 1 teaspoon of baking powder
- Salt and pepper to taste
- Olive oil for frying

Instructions:

1. Grate the zucchinis using a box grater or a food processor. Place the grated zucchini in a clean kitchen towel and squeeze out as much liquid as possible.
2. Finely chop the onion and garlic cloves.
3. In a large mixing bowl, combine the grated zucchini, chopped onion, garlic (if using), crumbled feta cheese (if using), chopped parsley or dill, eggs, flour, baking powder, salt, and pepper. Mix well until all ingredients are evenly incorporated.
4. Heat a few tablespoons of olive oil in a non-stick skillet over medium heat.
5. Spoon the zucchini mixture into the skillet, forming small pancakes. Flatten them slightly with the back of a spoon.
6. Cook the pancakes for 3-4 minutes on each side, or until golden brown and crispy. You may need to cook them in batches depending on the size of your skillet.
7. Once cooked, transfer the pancakes to a plate lined with paper towels to drain any excess oil.
8. Serve the zucchini pancakes hot, garnished with additional chopped parsley or dill if desired. You can enjoy them plain or with a side of yogurt or a dipping sauce of your choice.

These zucchini pancakes make a delicious appetizer, snack, or side dish. Enjoy!

Kısır (Turkish bulgur salad)

Ingredients:

- 1 cup fine bulgur
- 2 cups hot water
- 2 tablespoons tomato paste
- 1 tablespoon pepper paste (optional)
- 1 large tomato, diced
- 1 cucumber, diced
- 1 green bell pepper, finely chopped
- 3-4 green onions, finely chopped
- Half a bunch of parsley, finely chopped
- Half a bunch of fresh mint, finely chopped (optional)
- Juice of 1 lemon
- 3 tablespoons olive oil
- Salt and pepper to taste

Instructions:

1. Place the fine bulgur in a large bowl. Pour the hot water over the bulgur and let it sit for about 15-20 minutes until the bulgur absorbs the water and becomes soft. Fluff the bulgur with a fork occasionally.
2. In a separate bowl, mix together the tomato paste, pepper paste (if using), lemon juice, olive oil, salt, and pepper to make the dressing.
3. Add the diced tomato, cucumber, green bell pepper, green onions, parsley, and fresh mint (if using) to the softened bulgur.
4. Pour the dressing over the bulgur and vegetable mixture.
5. Mix everything together until well combined, using a spatula or spoon.
6. Transfer the kısır to a serving platter and garnish with additional parsley or mint leaves if desired.
7. Serve the kısır immediately or refrigerate for a while before serving. The flavors will develop more as it sits.

Kısır can be served as a side dish or as a standalone salad. Enjoy!

Fırın patates (Oven-roasted potatoes)

Ingredients:

- 1 kg (about 2 pounds) potatoes (you can use any variety suitable for roasting, such as Yukon Gold or Russet)
- 3-4 tablespoons olive oil
- 2-3 cloves of garlic, minced (optional)
- 1 teaspoon dried thyme (or any other herbs of your choice, such as rosemary or oregano)
- Salt and black pepper to taste
- Chopped fresh parsley for garnish (optional)

Instructions:

1. Preheat your oven to 200°C (400°F).
2. Wash the potatoes thoroughly and peel them if desired. Cut the potatoes into bite-sized cubes or wedges.
3. In a large mixing bowl, toss the potato cubes with olive oil, minced garlic (if using), dried thyme, salt, and black pepper. Make sure the potatoes are evenly coated with the seasoning.
4. Arrange the seasoned potatoes in a single layer on a baking sheet lined with parchment paper or aluminum foil. Make sure there is some space between each potato piece to ensure even cooking.
5. Place the baking sheet in the preheated oven and roast the potatoes for about 30-40 minutes, or until they are golden brown and crispy on the outside, and tender on the inside. Flip the potatoes halfway through the cooking time to ensure even browning.
6. Once the potatoes are cooked through and crispy, remove them from the oven and transfer them to a serving dish.
7. Garnish the oven-roasted potatoes with chopped fresh parsley (if using) and serve hot as a delicious side dish.

Enjoy your homemade oven-roasted potatoes! They pair well with a variety of main dishes and are always a crowd-pleaser.

Semizotu salatası (Purslane salad)

Ingredients:

- 2 cups fresh purslane leaves, washed and chopped
- 2 medium-sized tomatoes, diced
- 1 cucumber, diced
- 1/2 red onion, thinly sliced
- 1/4 cup chopped fresh parsley
- 1/4 cup chopped fresh mint
- Juice of 1 lemon
- 3 tablespoons extra virgin olive oil
- Salt and pepper to taste
- Optional: crumbled feta cheese or olives for garnish

Instructions:

1. Start by preparing the purslane leaves. Wash them thoroughly under cold water and remove any tough stems. Chop the leaves into bite-sized pieces and place them in a large salad bowl.
2. Add the diced tomatoes, cucumber, thinly sliced red onion, chopped parsley, and chopped mint to the bowl with the purslane.
3. In a small bowl, whisk together the lemon juice, extra virgin olive oil, salt, and pepper to make the dressing.
4. Pour the dressing over the salad ingredients in the bowl.
5. Toss the salad gently until all the ingredients are evenly coated with the dressing.
6. Taste the salad and adjust the seasoning if necessary by adding more salt, pepper, or lemon juice according to your preference.
7. If desired, garnish the purslane salad with crumbled feta cheese or olives for an extra burst of flavor.
8. Serve the salad immediately as a refreshing appetizer or side dish.

Purslane salad is best enjoyed fresh and can be served alongside grilled meats, fish, or as part of a mezze spread. Enjoy the unique flavor and texture of this nutritious green!

Fasulye piyazı (White bean salad)

Ingredients:

- 2 cups cooked white beans (canned beans are fine, just make sure to drain and rinse them)
- 1 small red onion, thinly sliced
- 2-3 tomatoes, diced
- 1/4 cup chopped fresh parsley
- 2-3 tablespoons extra virgin olive oil
- 1-2 tablespoons red wine vinegar or lemon juice
- 1 teaspoon ground cumin
- Salt and pepper to taste
- Optional: chopped green or red bell pepper, sliced green onions, olives, or boiled eggs for garnish

Instructions:

1. Start by preparing the white beans. If you're using canned beans, drain and rinse them under cold water. If you're using dried beans, cook them according to the package instructions until they are tender. Let the cooked beans cool down to room temperature.
2. In a large salad bowl, combine the cooked white beans, thinly sliced red onion, diced tomatoes, and chopped fresh parsley. If you're adding any optional ingredients like chopped bell pepper, green onions, or olives, add them to the salad bowl as well.
3. In a small bowl, whisk together the extra virgin olive oil, red wine vinegar or lemon juice, ground cumin, salt, and pepper to make the dressing.
4. Pour the dressing over the salad ingredients in the bowl.
5. Gently toss the salad until all the ingredients are evenly coated with the dressing.
6. Taste the salad and adjust the seasoning if necessary by adding more salt, pepper, or vinegar according to your preference.
7. If desired, garnish the white bean salad with additional chopped parsley and sliced boiled eggs.
8. Serve the salad immediately as a refreshing appetizer or side dish.

Fasulye piyazı is a versatile dish that can be served on its own as a light meal or as part of a mezze spread. Enjoy the flavors and textures of this delicious Turkish salad!

Meze tabağı (Assorted appetizers platter)

Ingredients:

For the Meze Selection:

- Hummus: A creamy chickpea dip made with tahini, lemon juice, garlic, and olive oil.
- Baba ghanoush: Smoky roasted eggplant dip flavored with tahini, garlic, lemon juice, and olive oil.
- Tzatziki: Refreshing yogurt dip with cucumber, garlic, dill, and mint.
- Muhammara: Spicy red pepper and walnut dip flavored with pomegranate molasses and spices.
- Olives: Assorted marinated olives, such as Kalamata or green olives stuffed with feta cheese.
- Dolma: Grape leaves stuffed with a flavorful mixture of rice, pine nuts, currants, and herbs.
- Cheese: Assorted cheeses like feta, halloumi, or Turkish white cheese.
- Turkish flatbread or pita bread: Cut into triangles or squares for dipping and scooping.

For Garnish:

- Fresh herbs: Sprigs of parsley, mint, or dill for garnish.
- Lemon wedges: Served on the side for squeezing over the dips.
- Extra virgin olive oil: Drizzle over the hummus and baba ghanoush for extra flavor.
- Sumac: Sprinkle over the hummus or tzatziki for a tangy, citrusy flavor (optional).

Instructions:

1. Arrange small bowls or plates on a large platter to hold each meze selection.
2. Fill each bowl or plate with the desired meze: hummus, baba ghanoush, tzatziki, muhammara, olives, dolma, and cheese.
3. Place the Turkish flatbread or pita bread on the platter, either in a separate bowl or arranged around the dips.
4. Garnish the platter with fresh herbs, lemon wedges, and a drizzle of extra virgin olive oil. Sprinkle sumac over the hummus or tzatziki if desired.

5. Serve the meze platter as an appetizer for sharing with friends and family. Provide small plates and utensils for serving.
6. Enjoy the assortment of flavors and textures, and feel free to customize the meze selection based on your preferences and availability of ingredients.

A meze platter is perfect for gatherings, parties, or as a light meal on its own. Serve with some refreshing drinks like Turkish tea, ayran (yogurt drink), or a glass of wine for a complete culinary experience.

Peynir tabağı (Assorted cheese platter)

Ingredients:

For the Cheese Selection:

- Feta cheese: A tangy and salty Greek cheese made from sheep's milk or a combination of sheep and goat milk.
- Turkish white cheese (Beyaz peynir): A brined white cheese with a crumbly texture and salty taste.
- Kasar cheese: A semi-hard Turkish cheese similar to mozzarella, with a mild and slightly tangy flavor.
- Tulum cheese: A traditional Turkish cheese aged in goat or sheepskin bags, known for its strong flavor and crumbly texture.
- Smoked cheese: A variety of cheese, such as smoked Gouda or smoked cheddar, for added depth of flavor.
- Blue cheese: A creamy and pungent cheese with blue veins running through it, such as Roquefort or Gorgonzola, for a bold taste.

For Garnish:

- Fresh fruits: Sliced fruits like grapes, figs, apples, or pears for a sweet contrast to the savory cheese.
- Nuts: Assorted nuts such as walnuts, almonds, or pistachios for added crunch and flavor.
- Honey: A drizzle of honey for pairing with the cheese, especially the blue cheese.
- Olives: Marinated olives, such as Kalamata or green olives, for a savory accompaniment.
- Crackers or bread: Assorted crackers, breadsticks, or crusty bread slices for serving alongside the cheese.

Instructions:

1. Arrange a selection of cheese on a large platter or cheese board, leaving space between each cheese to make it visually appealing.
2. Place each cheese variety on the platter, either whole or sliced, depending on your preference.

3. Garnish the cheese platter with fresh fruits, nuts, honey, and olives, arranging them around the cheese for an attractive presentation.
4. Add crackers or bread to the platter, either in a separate bowl or arranged alongside the cheese for serving.
5. Serve the cheese platter as an appetizer or as part of a cheese tasting experience. Provide cheese knives or spreaders for serving.
6. Encourage guests to mix and match different cheeses with fruits, nuts, and crackers to discover their favorite combinations.
7. Enjoy the assortment of flavors and textures, and feel free to customize the cheese selection based on your preferences and availability of cheeses.

A cheese platter is perfect for gatherings, parties, or as a sophisticated snack or appetizer. Pair it with some wine or sparkling water for a delightful culinary experience.

Şekerpare (Turkish semolina cookies soaked in syrup)

Ingredients:

For the Cookies:

- 1 cup semolina
- 1 cup all-purpose flour
- 1/2 cup unsalted butter, melted
- 1/2 cup powdered sugar
- 1 teaspoon baking powder
- 1/4 cup yogurt
- 1 teaspoon vanilla extract
- Whole blanched almonds or walnuts, for garnish (optional)

For the Syrup:

- 2 cups granulated sugar
- 2 cups water
- 1 tablespoon lemon juice
- 1 cinnamon stick or a few cloves (optional, for flavor)

Instructions:

1. Making the Syrup:

   1. In a saucepan, combine the granulated sugar, water, lemon juice, and cinnamon stick or cloves (if using).
   2. Bring the mixture to a boil over medium heat, stirring occasionally to dissolve the sugar.
   3. Once the sugar has dissolved, reduce the heat to low and let the syrup simmer for about 10-15 minutes, until it slightly thickens.
   4. Remove the saucepan from the heat and set aside to cool while you prepare the cookies.

2. Making the Cookies:

1. Preheat your oven to 180°C (350°F) and line a baking sheet with parchment paper.
2. In a mixing bowl, combine the melted butter and powdered sugar. Mix until well combined.
3. Add the semolina, all-purpose flour, baking powder, yogurt, and vanilla extract to the bowl. Mix until a soft dough forms.
4. Take small portions of the dough and shape them into small balls, about 1 inch in diameter. Place the balls on the prepared baking sheet, leaving some space between them.
5. If desired, gently press a whole blanched almond or walnut into the center of each cookie for garnish.
6. Bake the cookies in the preheated oven for 15-20 minutes, or until they are lightly golden brown on the bottom.
7. Remove the cookies from the oven and let them cool slightly on the baking sheet.

3. Assembling the Şekerpare:

1. Once the cookies have cooled slightly, transfer them to a serving dish or plate.
2. Pour the cooled syrup over the warm cookies, allowing them to absorb the syrup. You can use a spoon to drizzle the syrup over the cookies evenly.
3. Let the şekerpare sit for at least 1-2 hours, allowing the cookies to soak up the syrup and become soft and delicious.
4. Serve the şekerpare at room temperature, garnished with additional nuts or shredded coconut if desired.

Enjoy your homemade şekerpare! These sweet and syrupy cookies are sure to be a hit with family and friends.

Baklava (Layers of phyllo pastry filled with nuts and honey)

Ingredients:

- 1 package of phyllo pastry sheets
- 2 cups of mixed nuts (such as pistachios, walnuts, and almonds), chopped
- 1 cup of unsalted butter, melted
- 1 cup of granulated sugar
- 1 cup of water
- 1/2 cup of honey
- 1 teaspoon of ground cinnamon (optional)
- 1 teaspoon of vanilla extract (optional)

Instructions:

1. Preheat your oven to 180°C (350°F). Grease a baking dish with butter.
2. In a bowl, mix together the chopped nuts with cinnamon (if using).
3. Lay one sheet of phyllo pastry in the greased baking dish and brush it with melted butter. Repeat with several more sheets of phyllo, brushing each layer with butter.
4. Spread a layer of the chopped nuts mixture evenly over the phyllo pastry.
5. Continue layering phyllo pastry sheets and brushing with butter, followed by another layer of nuts, until all the nuts are used.
6. Finish with a final layer of phyllo pastry sheets, brushing each sheet with butter.
7. Using a sharp knife, cut the baklava into diamond or square shapes.
8. Bake in the preheated oven for about 30-35 minutes, or until the baklava is golden brown and crisp.
9. While the baklava is baking, prepare the syrup. In a saucepan, combine the sugar, water, honey, and vanilla extract (if using). Bring to a boil, then reduce the heat and simmer for about 10 minutes, until slightly thickened.
10. Once the baklava is done baking, remove it from the oven and immediately pour the hot syrup over the hot baklava.
11. Allow the baklava to cool completely in the baking dish before serving. This allows the syrup to soak into the pastry layers.
12. Serve the baklava at room temperature and enjoy!

Künefe (Turkish cheese pastry soaked in syrup)

Ingredients:

- 500g shredded phyllo dough (kataifi)
- 250g mozzarella cheese, shredded
- 1 cup of unsalted butter, melted
- 1 cup of granulated sugar
- 1 cup of water
- 1/2 cup of honey
- Crushed pistachios or ground cinnamon for garnish (optional)

Instructions:

1. Preheat your oven to 180°C (350°F). Grease a round baking dish with butter.
2. In a bowl, mix together the shredded mozzarella cheese with a bit of melted butter.
3. Spread half of the shredded phyllo dough in the bottom of the greased baking dish.
4. Spread the cheese mixture evenly over the layer of phyllo dough.
5. Cover the cheese layer with the remaining shredded phyllo dough, pressing down gently.
6. Drizzle the remaining melted butter over the top of the künefe.
7. Bake in the preheated oven for about 30-35 minutes, or until the künefe is golden brown and crisp.
8. While the künefe is baking, prepare the syrup. In a saucepan, combine the sugar, water, and honey. Bring to a boil, then reduce the heat and simmer for about 10 minutes, until slightly thickened.
9. Once the künefe is done baking, remove it from the oven and immediately pour the hot syrup over the hot künefe.
10. Allow the künefe to cool slightly before serving. Garnish with crushed pistachios or ground cinnamon if desired.
11. Serve the künefe warm and enjoy the sweet, cheesy goodness!

These traditional Turkish desserts are sure to impress with their rich flavors and textures. Enjoy making and sharing them with your loved ones!

Revani (Semolina cake soaked in syrup)

Ingredients:

For the Cake:

- 1 cup fine semolina
- 1 cup all-purpose flour
- 1 cup granulated sugar
- 1 cup plain yogurt
- 1/2 cup vegetable oil or melted butter
- 3 eggs
- Zest of 1 lemon or orange (optional)
- 1 teaspoon baking powder
- 1/2 teaspoon vanilla extract (optional)

For the Syrup:

- 1 cup granulated sugar
- 1 cup water
- Juice of 1 lemon

Instructions:

1. Making the Cake:

    1. Preheat your oven to 180°C (350°F). Grease a 9x13 inch baking dish with butter or oil.
    2. In a large mixing bowl, beat together the eggs and sugar until pale and fluffy.
    3. Add the yogurt, vegetable oil or melted butter, and vanilla extract (if using), and mix until well combined.
    4. In a separate bowl, whisk together the semolina, flour, baking powder, and lemon or orange zest (if using).
    5. Gradually add the dry ingredients to the wet ingredients, mixing until you have a smooth batter.

6. Pour the batter into the prepared baking dish and spread it out evenly.
7. Bake in the preheated oven for 25-30 minutes, or until the cake is golden brown and a toothpick inserted into the center comes out clean.

2. Making the Syrup:

1. While the cake is baking, prepare the syrup. In a saucepan, combine the sugar, water, and lemon juice.
2. Bring the mixture to a boil over medium heat, stirring occasionally to dissolve the sugar.
3. Once the sugar has dissolved, reduce the heat to low and let the syrup simmer for about 10 minutes, until slightly thickened.

3. Assembling the Revani:

1. Once the cake is done baking, remove it from the oven and let it cool slightly in the baking dish.
2. While the cake is still warm, use a knife to cut it into diamond or square shapes.
3. Slowly pour the hot syrup over the warm cake, allowing it to soak in. You may need to do this in batches to ensure that the cake absorbs the syrup evenly.
4. Let the Revani cool completely in the baking dish before serving.

4. Serving:

1. Once cooled, transfer the Revani to a serving platter.
2. Garnish with chopped nuts or shredded coconut if desired.
3. Serve the Revani at room temperature and enjoy!

Revani is a deliciously moist and flavorful dessert that's perfect for any occasion. Enjoy making and sharing it with your loved ones!

Lokma (Turkish fried dough balls soaked in syrup)

Ingredients:

For the Dough:

- 1 cup lukewarm water
- 1 tablespoon active dry yeast
- 1 teaspoon granulated sugar
- 2 cups all-purpose flour
- Pinch of salt
- Vegetable oil for frying

For the Syrup:

- 2 cups granulated sugar
- 1 1/2 cups water
- Juice of 1 lemon
- 1 cinnamon stick or a few cloves (optional)

Instructions:

1. Making the Dough:

   1. In a small bowl, mix together the lukewarm water, active dry yeast, and granulated sugar. Let it sit for about 5-10 minutes, until the yeast becomes frothy.
   2. In a large mixing bowl, sift the all-purpose flour and add a pinch of salt.
   3. Pour the activated yeast mixture into the flour and mix until a smooth dough forms. The dough should be soft and slightly sticky.
   4. Cover the bowl with a clean kitchen towel or plastic wrap and let the dough rise in a warm place for about 1-2 hours, until it doubles in size.

2. Making the Syrup:

1. While the dough is rising, prepare the syrup. In a saucepan, combine the granulated sugar, water, lemon juice, and cinnamon stick or cloves (if using).
2. Bring the mixture to a boil over medium heat, stirring occasionally to dissolve the sugar.
3. Once the sugar has dissolved, reduce the heat to low and let the syrup simmer for about 10-15 minutes, until it slightly thickens. Remove from heat and set aside to cool.

3. Frying the Dough:

1. Heat vegetable oil in a deep frying pan or pot over medium heat.
2. Using a spoon or a small scoop, carefully drop small portions of the risen dough into the hot oil. Be cautious not to overcrowd the pan.
3. Fry the dough balls until they are golden brown and crispy on the outside, and cooked through on the inside. This should take about 2-3 minutes per batch.
4. Use a slotted spoon to remove the fried dough balls from the oil and transfer them to a plate lined with paper towels to drain any excess oil.

4. Soaking in Syrup:

1. While the Lokma are still warm, immerse them in the prepared syrup, making sure they are fully coated.
2. Let the Lokma soak in the syrup for a few minutes, allowing them to absorb the sweetness.
3. Remove the Lokma from the syrup and transfer them to a serving platter.

5. Serving:

1. Serve the Lokma warm or at room temperature.
2. Garnish with chopped nuts or shredded coconut if desired.
3. Enjoy these delicious Turkish fried dough balls soaked in syrup as a sweet treat!

Lokma is best enjoyed fresh, but they can also be stored in an airtight container at room temperature for up to a day. Enjoy making and sharing this delightful dessert with family and friends!